Fore All Golfers!

Inspirations & rules to improve your game
and help you overall in the game of golf.

By Lionell "Buddy" Spretz

Fore All Golfers!

Library of Congress
Cataloging-in-Publication Data
ISBN 1-56167-779-5
Library of Congress Card Catalog Number:
2002094690
Second Printing

Published by

American Literary Press, Inc.
Five Star Special Edition
8019 Belair Road, Suite 10
Baltimore, Maryland 21236

Manufactured in the United States of America

This book is dedicated first to the Lord Jesus, who gave me the wisdom to remember and think of the sayings and ideas, and secondly to my wife, who helped me with this entire booklet for the eight to ten months that it took to think of it, write it and complete it.

Lionell "Buddy" Spretz

Introduction

This book is for beginners, intermediates and single digit handicappers. Yes, it is for everyone. After you read this book, which should take about one hour, you will know more about golf and golf etiquette than 70% of all golfers. Everything written here is to improve your game and to help you overall.

Several things are repeated, the reason being, THEY ARE IMPORTANT! I have been playing golf for 35 years and these are some of the mistakes I have seen dozens of people make. Please try to apply these simple sayings to your game. If your children want to start playing golf, have them read this book first.

If you are a beginner - Start by taking some lessons from a teaching professional.

If you start playing and doing it right from the beginning, you WILL become a much better golfer than the person who doesn't take the lessons.

Learn the rules of golf.

If you know the rules, you will probably be the only one in your foursome who does.

Read this book more than once.

This book, although not long, is taken from years of experience and from watching people make mistake after mistake.

Slow play is for 115 year old men
and women.

If you're playing slow, pick up
your ball, write down a 7 or 8 on
your scorecard and move on
to the next hole.

Always have fun.

If you're throwing clubs, cursing,
or drinking heavily your blood
pressure will more than likely
be up, and if that's true,
you can't have fun.

How come the more you practice, the luckier you get and the better your score becomes?

Lucky - Lucky - Lucky!

Have your putt already lined up
by the time it is your turn to putt.

This can't always happen, but it
will save time when it's possible.
Also, always putt out if you're
not standing or walking in someone else's line.

<u>Play</u> <u>ready</u> <u>golf</u> - You don't have to rush, but if no one in your group is in your way, hit out of turn, so to speak.

Make sure you have agreed on this with the other golfers in your group at the #1 tee.

Turn in all your scores when establishing a handicap.

YES, even the low ones!

Always take enough club to get the ball to the green (hole) with your normal swing.

No big deal if you're hitting a 5 iron and your playing partner is hitting a 7 iron. You got to the green and they didn't.

<u>Never</u> drink a lot of alcoholic beverages while playing golf.

Only a FOOL drives after drinking. Believe me when I say this, very few people want to be seen with a FOOL.

When you have a water hazard
to go over, always make sure
you have enough club to
get over the water.

It is very difficult to hit your next
shot out of six feet of water.

If you are having some troubles with your game - TAKE A LESSON FROM A GOOD TEACHING PROFESSIONAL.

Yes, I am a teaching professional, and I know what I am talking about.

Never slam your club into the ground or into anything else.

Not only is it dangerous, but no one likes to play golf with someone who loses their temper. No one is that good to be acting that way anyhow.

Don't move around when others
are hitting or putting.

Have the same consideration for
your fellow golfers as they have
for you.

Please do not drag your shoes on
the green.

If you accidentally do, repair it
for the next group, the group in
front of you did it for you.

If you hit your ball close to out of bounds and you have an idea it might have gone out of bounds...

...hit another ball (provisional), just in case, to save time.

Please replace all divots with sand or the original divot.

If you do, others will see you and will do likewise. You know how hard it is to hit out of a divot.

If you are not playing in a
tournament, putt out all
putts even those 6-8 inches
from the hole.

Other people have
seen you putt.

Never drive your golf cart too fast or recklessly.

Save this for the race track.

Do not let small children drive golf carts.

Also, don't let them drive your car.

Make sure your ball is marked
so you can identify it.

Have your own unique
ball marks.

After finishing nine (9) holes, do not take a long time in the snack bar.

If you have a sandwich, either eat it very quickly or take it on the back nine with you.

After you hit and your club is either dirty or you have your head cover in your hand, sit in the cart and wait until you get to your next shot.

This will keep the group behind you from hitting into you.

Never take over five (5) minutes looking for your ball.

If you are dead set on finding your ball, then let the group behind you play through.

Don't look for other balls in the water or rough, unless it is yours or someone in your group's ball...

...then refer back to rule #25.

Practice - Practice - Practice!

But make sure you are
practicing the right way.

Never urinate in public.

By the way, this is against
the law.

Always have fun!

This is not the way you make a living, so, again, I say, Have Fun!

Amateurs and weekend golfers...don't take the game real seriously.

When we get on the tour, that's when we can become real serious about the game.

Never use foul language
(out loud).

It makes you look like a fool.
Using foul language is
disgusting anyway.

Never tell your playing partners
what to do or how to play
a shot...

...if they haven't asked.

Do not walk in your playing
partners' line on the green.

It can change the direction
of the putt.

Finish out putting if you are not walking in your playing partners' line.

This will give you more time.

Keep golf carts well away
from the green.

You don't drive your car on
your yard, do you?

Keep pull carts off the fringe and off of the greens.

You don't pull it through your house on your carpet, DO YOU?

Take lessons from a good
teaching professional.

Yes, I am a professional teacher,
but the truth is, good teaching
professionals <u>can</u> improve
your game.

Always take an extra club with you when you walk to your ball, especially if you are unsure of the distance...

...two or three clubs, if necessary.

Always rake the sand trap after
you hit and walk out of it.

The person before you did
it or should have.

Don't hit into or rush the players in front of you.

Make sure they are out of range. If you hit into the players in front of you, you may have to fight all of them. <u>By Yourself</u>.

Always dress properly, not like you've been sleeping in your clothes.

Keeping your shoes and clubs clean will also help. You might be surprised how it will improve your game.

Always drink plenty of water in hot weather.

It's hard to hit your second shot laying on your back.

Never stand directly behind someone while they are hitting.

Try to stand at least 20 feet or more away from them.

Always use the 90 degree rule
when driving a golf cart
in the fairways.

On most par 3's you must keep
the cart on the cart path
at all times.

Repair all ball marks on the green.

The people in front of you did. If your ball hits one while putting, it tends to alter the direction of the ball.

Turn in your correct score,
low or high.

If you are a sandbagger, every
time you look at the prize or tro-
phy you won, it will only remind
you of the time you cheated.

A sandbagger is one who LIES
about the scores they turn in.

A sandbagger is also considered
a cheat

Always ask your playing partners if they need the pin tended.

Never lay the pin where any golf ball might accidentally hit it.

Have your own clubs.

You would be surprised how many times two people play out of one bag.

Tee up your ball on all par 3's.

It is easier to hit the ball from
a tee.

Get to your tee time on time.

It is rude to your playing partners
to be late.

When you finish a hole, do not write your score on the card until you get to the next tee box.

This will save time. Watch how many people do this and how much extra time it takes.

Never speed in the golf cart.

This can be very dangerous.

Pay for a less fortunate person's
green fee three or four
times a year.

You will always remember the
look of happiness on their face.

Try to get to the golf course early
enough to warm up by hitting
some range balls.

I really know this will save you
three or four strokes a round
or more.

Never hit mulligans if someone is behind you.

How would you feel if you were the one waiting?

Always keep your eye on your ball and also on your playing partners' balls.

This will save time.

Yell FORE!!

If there is any doubt about coming close to someone, yell FORE. Better safe, than sorry. If you don't, you could seriously injure someone.

Before you take a practice
swing...

...make sure no one is behind or
near you.

God made all the heavens and
the earth...

...enjoy your surroundings while
playing golf.

If your grips on your clubs are slick, be sure to replace them soon.

It will also allow you to hit the ball better.

When you play golf, hit the ball hard, and it will become a habit.

I'm not talking about busting your shoe laces every shot. In other words, DO NOT DECELERATE!

The more you practice something wrong, the worse you become.

The more you practice something right, the better you become. Yes, I say again, if your game is hurting, let a Professional Golf Teacher help you.

If you can't control your driver,
hit a 3 wood off of the tee box...

...at least until a teaching
professional gets you hitting
the driver correctly.

Practice your chipping and putting frequently. This is 68% of the game.

But you know what? You need to be able to put the ball in the short grass from the tee.

While watching golf on
television...

...pay attention to the players'
swings and watch how they hit
the ball first and then
take a divot.

Have fun - this is NOT your livelihood.

When you get home, whether you've had a bad or good game, go eat and to a movie with your spouse and tell them how much you love them. If you're single, take a friend and just have fun.

If you are a high handicapper,
stop thinking about your swing so
much, and just hit the ball.

If you are a low handicapper, stop
thinking about your swing so
much, and just hit the ball.

If you really want to improve your game, go to someone who knows the game, a good teaching professional.

Only about 15% of all golfers have had some lessons.

Keep your score cards.

This enables you to check your progress over the next few months and years.

Get the ball on the green ASAP.

If you are only a short distance off the green and you have a lot of green to the hole, use a 6 or 7 iron, not a wedge. The saying is Minimum Air Time - Maximum Ground Time for this shot.

Never play with someone that criticizes you.

You probably get enough of that at work.

Always be the best sportsman or sportswoman on and off the course.

Never brag about yourself, but always about others.

When you approach the ball to hit it, have confidence, and then hit it.

If doubt enters your mind, back off and then approach the shot again, this time with confidence.

Golf is just the KISS Rule.

If you don't know what that is,
put this book down now and ask
someone in your house or call a
friend and ask them what the
KISS Rule is.

If you already have eight or nine strokes on a hole and a group is behind you...

...pick up and let your group finish while you are waiting at the golf cart. Always keep up with your group.

If a sand trap is 230 yards out and it would be your career shot to get over it, hit a 3 or 4 wood.

Laying up is no sin, it's smart.

When you approach your ball to hit, have your mind made up.

You know your game - Don't let someone else talk you into hitting the wrong club.

Don't lie about your score.

You might be surprised how many people know that you're doing it. Besides, you're hurting yourself more than anyone else.

Never throw your clubs.

It only makes YOU look like an IDIOT.

Never hit a tree, a pole or
anything hard with your clubs
on purpose.

How STUPID IS THIS?!

Stay in shape, mainly keep your
weight under control.

You will be surprised how much
better you feel and how much
better you will play.

If you have more than one hole open in front of you and the group behind you is pushing (rushing) you, let them play through (go ahead of you).

If you don't, you'll be sorry, because it will effect your game.

Don't try to fix your own golf swing.

Have a professional golf teacher help you. Don't brag about not ever taking a lesson. no wonder you don't get any better.

Play the game the way <u>you</u> play...

...not to your opponent's play.

Remember, this game is not how you make a living...

...this is for fun.

If you have to make or receive a phone call,drop out of the hole,go where your playing partners' can't hear you.

DO NOT hold them up or hold up the group behind you,

Always think positively while playing golf.

This will probably save you 4 to 8 strokes a round.

Always play more break than you think on a putt...

...especially if the green is very fast.

Don't rush the group in front of
you just because you are
in a hurry.

Remember how it feels when
someone behind you is
rushing you.

Always wear a hat in the sun.

And don't forget about sunscreen.

Always wear sunglasses in
the sun.

Also, because you are outside a
lot longer than normal, have your
eyes checked regularly.

Always have bandaids and aspirins with you.

You never know when they might come in handy.

Always move your ball out of a ground crack or a hole.

Remember, this is just for fun for most of us. It's also within the rules

Always move your ball away
from tree roots.

Hitting the shot on or by the roots
could be very dangerous. This
could also damage your club.
Exception to this is if you are
in a tournament.

Always conduct yourself as a
gentleman or a lady.

Someone is always watching.

Do not lose your temper.

It makes you look like a fool.
NO ONE LIKES A FOOL.

While tending the pin for some-one, hold the flag so it doesn't blow in the wind.

I am referring to the cloth part, not just the pole.

Before you tend the pin, take the pin out and lean it backwards...

....so it doesn't get stuck in the hole.

Practice the shots you need help on much more than the others...

...but remember, don't practice unless you have taken a lesson and know what you are doing wrong.

In this order - take some lessons, practice and play, take another lesson or two, practice and play keeping up the routine for awhile and you'll be shooting the score you've dreamed about.

You will advance your game far beyond your expectations.

Greg Norman never played golf until he was 19 years old, but he did take lessons and he did practice.

A LOT!

All golf lessons aren't real
expensive - shop around.

There are lots of teachers that are
very reasonable and still
very good.

You are never too young or too
old to start playing golf...

...or too little, or too big.

No matter how good you become...

...you must practice to stay good.

Always lay the extra club you take to the green in the path of the golf cart so you have to walk by it on the way back to the cart.

That way you will not leave or lose your club.

Never lay the pin down so that
the ball might run into it.

If you hit the pin, this results
in a penalty.

Customers really like to
play golf.

I play golf with customers about
40 times a year, and where else
can you talk to a customer for
three or four hours?

When the sun is out, WEAR SUNSCREEN...

...this could save your life.

If you are 10 - 20 yards off the green and the pin is on the front, use a wedge.

The saying is "maximum air time, minimum ground time".

Keep your voice down on the golf course.

Think about how irritated you get when someone is too loud.

Anyone can say they can tell you how to play golf or tell you what you are doing wrong.

Ask them for their teaching certification.

Just because a golf instructor charges a lot doesn't mean they know what they are doing.

You should be comfortable with the teacher.

Everyone knows what you mean when you say the ball went straight, but do they understand...

A fade is a ball that goes a little right, a slice a lot right, a draw goes a little left, and a hook goes a lot to the left. This is opposite for left handed golfers.

When tending the pin, make sure you hold the cloth flag, not just the pin.

It keeps the flag from flapping in the wind.

There are several things that golfers must do to become better, but the main one is Practice.

Always aim at something when practicing. Always practice with a purpose.

To get the ball high, hit down on the ball.

This will get it up higher and quicker.

When taking a lesson from a good teaching professional, ask him what you need to do to become a better player.

Trust me, he will tell you.

Always visualize your shot before you hit the ball, whether it is with your driver, an iron, a wedge or a putter.

Think where you want the ball to go and then hit it.

Remember, the better you look...

...the better you feel and the
better you play.

Never decelerate on any shot.

In other words, do not start fast
on your down swing and then
slow down before you
hit the ball.

While putting, do not move anything except your arms, wrist,
shoulders and hands.

Use the pendulum swing.

If you are a fivesome...

...let faster players play through.

Throw trash into trash bins...

...not onto the course.

Stay in shape, or get into shape.

You will play better golf.

Playing golf with someone who's better than you will help you play better in the future.

You may be able to pick up some tips from them.

Always have an extra ball in your pocket.

This will save time.

90% of all putts that are short will not go in.

This study was done by your local college.

Practice, Practice, Practice...

...But if you're not practicing right, you're hurting your game instead of helping it.

Just because you play badly
sometimes it may not be you.

It could be your equipment. Yes,
the right equipment does make
a difference

Don't feed the animals you see
on the course from your hand,
especially the squirrels.

They don't know where the
food chain stops.

My suggestion is that NO HUSBAND tells or teaches his WIFE how to play golf.

There are already too many divorces.

You play golf for fun and exercise. Your average score is about 150 per 18 holes.

WHY are you teaching your child how to play golf? Why not assist your doctor in the operating room?

If you buy two (2) mulligans at a fundraiser...

...please don't take four, six or even eight while you're playing.

The person who brags about
never taking a lesson and never
practicing, doesn't have to brag
about it.

We can tell.

About 3% of the best golfers
need to be hitting from
the back tees.

Why are you hitting from the
back tees? Are you in
the top 3%?

My reason for writing this short booklet has been twofold:

>   1. When people know golf etiquette and the rules, they have more fun on the golf course and they don't take all day playing.

>   2. I hope to make enough money off the sales of this book to quit my job and go into teaching golf full time. I am a certified golf teacher now.

Always have this book on the golf course with you.

Lastly, there are many more things you can do to make the game easier and a lot more fun. Enjoy this game. Don't get mad, and the best way to improve is to practice - practice, and take some lessons and then practice and play.

Good Luck and Keep Them In The Fairway!

Buddy's book is creative in the sense of pin pointing etiquette that is truly abused on the golf course. This little book reminds players of simple principles that you know but sometimes forget to take into consideration, such as good course management and percentages.

—Alex Osmond III, Head Pro, Bay Forest GC

Buddy's book is a must for everyone beginning golf and is at the same time especially for the corporate golfer who needs to impress his or her boss and/or clients. Reading this book and applying the principles can be a great way to avoid embarrassing situations. A movie should be made from this book.

—Fred Marti, Director of Golf, Evergreen Point GC

For information on bulk orders, contact

American Literary Press, Inc.
8019 Belair Rd. • Baltimore, Maryland 21236
(410) 882-7700 • 1-800-873-2003 out of area
www.erols.com/amerlit